Pictured above: A red-eyed tree frog at home in a rain forest • *On the front and back cover:* a lightning storm over a city • *On the end pages (pp. 2-3 & 110-111):* A lightning storm over Cape Town, South Africa • *On the title page:* Computer-enhanced images of actual snowflakes

WONDERS OF WEATHER

by
Frances Nankin

Scientific consultant:

Gary A. England
Chief Meteorologist, KWTV
Chief Meteorologist, Mediavergence, Inc.
Consulting Meteorologist, Weather Designs, Inc.
American Meteorological Society

Kidsbooks®

Introduction

No matter where we go or what we do, weather plays a part in our lives. Even if you rarely think about the weather, it affects the world around you. Weather influences the design of the clothes we wear, of the buildings we live and work in, of the cars and other vehicles we travel in, and much more. It also affects many decisions that we make every day: Do I play outside or stay in? Will I ride my bike to school or get a ride? Should I wear a T-shirt or take a sweater?

Weather, however, is not just something that we deal with because we have to. Observing and trying to predict the weather is a fun, fascinating, and ever-changing activity. You don't have to be a meteorologist (a scientist who studies weather) to find excitement and beauty in what is happening in the air around you.

This book will introduce you to many key elements and effects of weather. It will help you know what to look for, and to understand how and why it happens. At the back of the book, you will find a glossary that provides explanations of terms that might be unfamiliar.

Are you ready to enter the world of weather?

This bright-orange ball is a photograph of our sun, a star made of burning, exploding gases. The sun's temperature is so intense that no life can exist on it. Without it, however, there would be no weather on Earth—and no life, either.

Contents

What Is Weather?

The next time you go outside, look up. Imagine that you are standing at the bottom of a deep sea of air. What is going on up there? Thinking about weather means thinking about Earth's air: how hot or cold it is, how wet or dry, how windy or still.

Knowing the weather forecast can mean the difference between life and death if a blizzard's blinding snowfall, a hurricane's relentless downpour, or a tornado's terrifying blast is headed your way.

Most of the time, we pay no attention to what the air outside is doing. But when we have to decide which clothes to put on or what the day's activities will be, we begin to realize how much weather affects all of us, in almost every aspect of our lives.

8

Studies have shown that the human body is affected by weather. Headaches or aching joints, for instance, can be signs of an approaching storm. Aches and pains often occur when weather changes quickly, such as when the temperature suddenly drops or the air gets heavy and damp.

Q&A
Does weather affect our mood?
Apparently so. In a survey conducted by a TV weather station recently, more than seven out of ten people said that the weather directly affects how they feel, physically and mentally.

What Is Climate?

Weather is a short-term condition. In most places, it changes from day to day, week to week, and season to season. *Climate*, however, is a long-term condition—the kind of weather that a region tends to have over many years (30 or more), including average temperatures and long-term totals for rainfall, sunshine, and wind conditions.

Most people live in temperate climates—where summers are warm, winters are cold, and rain falls in regular patterns. Humans can survive in almost any climate, as long as they know what to expect, and build homes and wear clothes best suited to those conditions.

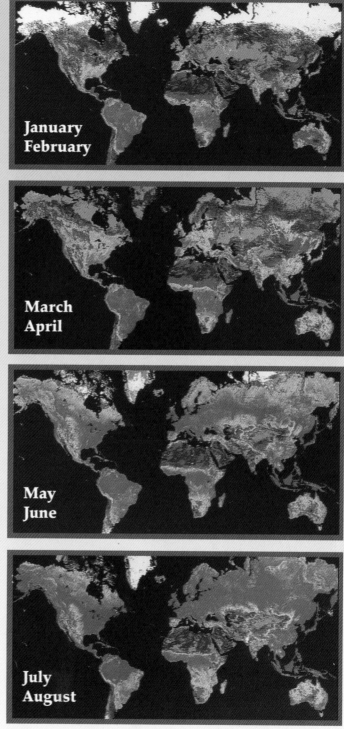

January
February

March
April

May
June

July
August

These satellite photos were taken at different times in a one-year weather cycle. Note which regions are snowy (white) most of the year, which are always dry (brown), and which show change as the year progresses.

Animals and plants that have adapted to their habitat's climate usually thrive. The emperor penguin lives in Antarctica, in the coldest climate on Earth. The bird's thick coat of feathers helps it survive in temperatures as low as -80°F (-62°C) and icy winds up to 100 miles per hour.

Rain forests and deserts have different climates, even though both are usually hot year-round. A rain forest's lush plant growth holds moisture in the soil and puts it back into the air. Any rain a desert gets is soaked up by the dry soil or evaporates in the hot air before it hits the ground.

The Sun

We usually think of weather as what is going on outside our own door. The main reason we have weather, though, is nearly 93 million miles away—the sun. It plays a key part in every type of weather on Earth.

DID YOU KNOW . . . ?

• The sun—the closest star to Earth—is 92,980,000 miles away from us.

• The sun's radius (distance from center to surface) is about 432,500 miles. The sun takes up as much space as 1.3 million Earths put together!

• The sun is about 27,000,000°F (14,999,982°C) at its core and about 10,000°F (5,538°C) at its surface. The sun has no real surface, however; it is all gas. Any solids or liquids there would be burned up instantly.

• The sun's light travels through space at 186,000 miles per second. It takes 8.3 minutes to reach Earth.

The sun's superhot temperatures come from nuclear reactions at its core. A nuclear reaction occurs when tiny atomic particles collide and turn into energy, giving off intense heat and light. The sun's core has enough atomic particles to burn for billions of years.

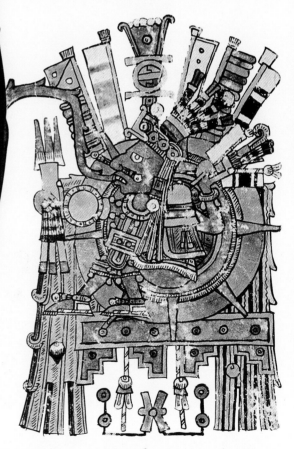

This is Tonatiuh, sun god of the Aztecs of ancient Mexico. He was also an eagle. Aztecs called the morning sun "the eagle that rises" and the evening sun "the eagle that falls."

How the Sun Causes Weather

The sun is the main reason Earth has weather.

The sun heats Earth's oceans and land, which warm the air. This heating is uneven, however, and that is what keeps Earth's air moving. You can see the same kind of motion in a pot of water as it starts to boil. Warmer water rises while cooler water sinks, making swirling currents. Earth's air currents are put in motion the same way.

Earth keeps the same tilt as it orbits the sun. This is what causes changing seasons. When the Northern Hemisphere is tilted closer to the sun, it has summer and the Southern Hemisphere has winter. The opposite is true when the Southern Hemisphere is tilted closer to the sun's rays.

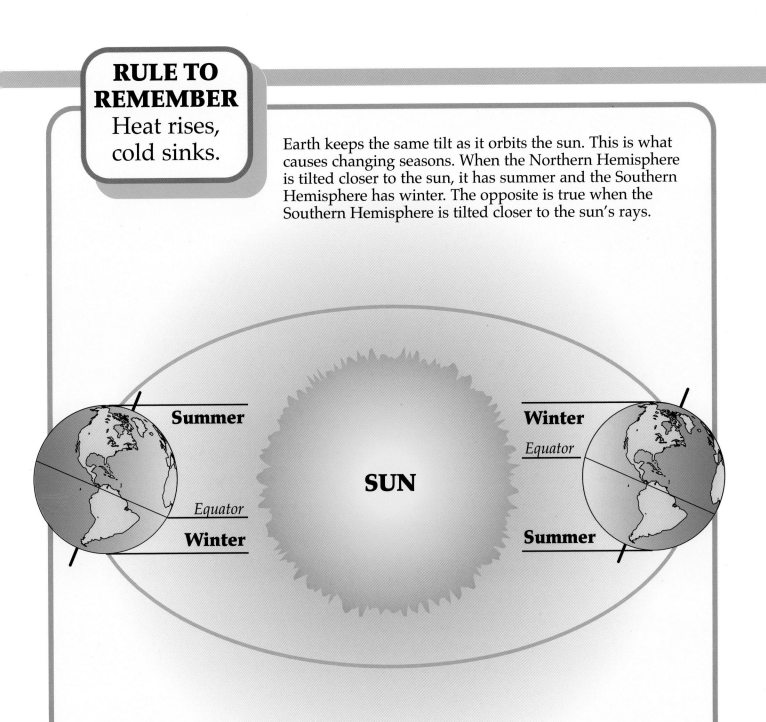

As Earth orbits the sun, water and land near the equator get the sun's most direct rays. It is hot there year-round. In the Northern or Southern Hemispheres, the sun's rays hit Earth's surface at an angle, so the heat is less intense. In summer, when the rays are more direct, we feel the heat. During winter, the sun stays low in the sky and it doesn't feel as hot.

Earth has different types of surfaces, which is another reason for the uneven heating of its air. Dark surfaces, such as forests, absorb more heat than light surfaces do. (You can feel cooler by wearing light-colored clothes in summer; warmer by wearing dark colors in winter.) Snowy and icy surfaces stay cool because they reflect heat and light away. The air above dark surfaces gets warmer than the air above light surfaces.

Earth's Blanket of Air

Earth is surrounded by a blanket of air, or atmosphere. Our atmosphere has five layers, each different from the one above it.

Earth's atmosphere acts like a blanket, holding in some of the sun's warmth. Without it, parts of Earth facing away from the sun would rapidly lose all the warmth gained during the day. That is what happens on the moon, which has no atmosphere. The moon's sunlit side is about 250°F (121°C)—hotter than boiling water—while its dark side is -290°F (-179°C)!

WORDS FOR THE WISE

Each layer of Earth's atmosphere has a descriptive name. A *sphere* is a specific place or area; the prefixes tell you more. *Tropo-* means "change"; *strato-* means "layer"; *meso-* means "middle"; *thermo-* means "heat"; and *exo-* means "outer" or "outside."

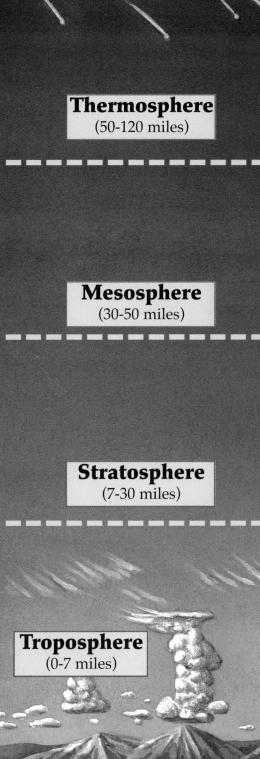

Exosphere
(120-600 miles)

Thermosphere
(50-120 miles)

Mesosphere
(30-50 miles)

Stratosphere
(7-30 miles)

Troposphere
(0-7 miles)

We live in the troposphere, where most weather—clouds, rain, and wind—occurs. Jet planes usually fly higher, in the stratosphere, to avoid dangerous weather conditions, such as thunderstorms.

On some clear, dark nights, people who live far north or far south can see shimmering curtains of color high in the sky. This breathtaking display is called the aurora borealis (northern lights) in the Northern Hemisphere and aurora australis (southern lights) in the Southern Hemisphere. It occurs when particles given off by the sun interact with particles in Earth's thermosphere or exosphere, where the air is very thin.

The outermost layer of Earth's atmosphere is the hottest. Temperatures there range from about 570°F (300°C) to above 3,000°F (1,650°C). The mesosphere is the coldest layer, getting as low as -150°F (-101.1°C).

Meteors—those space rocks sometimes called shooting stars—make their fiery streaks across the sky because of Earth's atmosphere, which acts like a shield: Few rocks reach the ground, because they burn up as they pass through the air.

What Else Causes Weather?

Earth sometimes interacts with its atmosphere in ways that change the weather. For instance, an erupting volcano can pump huge amounts of ash and dust into the atmosphere, forming a vast cloud that can circle the planet and block the sun's rays.

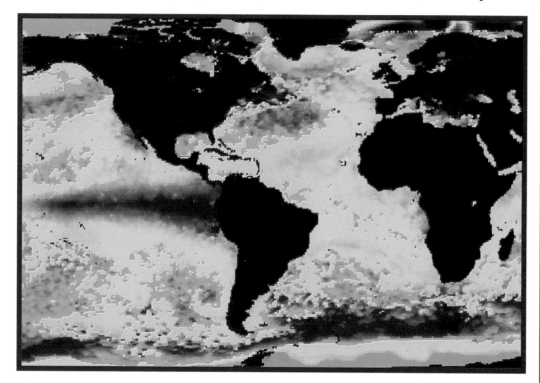

The dark-red streak off South America's west *(left)* coast shows the location of an El Niño—an area of Pacific Ocean waters that are warmer than usual.

El Niño is an area of warmer-than-usual water that sometimes occurs in the Pacific Ocean off South America. An El Niño can change weather patterns in its area, which can set off unusual weather worldwide, such as heavy rains where it is usually dry and drought where it is normally rainy.

20

On calm, clear nights, temperatures in big cities can measure as much as 18°F (10°C) higher than surrounding areas. The many buildings and streets hold the sun's heat. Extra heat is created by heaters, air-conditioners, lighting, automobile exhaust, and other devices.

The huge 1815 eruption of Mount Tambora, Indonesia, may be to blame for the "year without summer" of 1816. That year, parts of Europe and North America suffered snow and frost during June, July, and August!

The 1991 eruption of Mount Pinatubo in the Philippines (*at left*) sent so much sulfur dioxide gas into the atmosphere that a thin haze formed worldwide. That haze may have been responsible for the cooler-than-normal summer in 1992.

Air On the Move

Wind is the movement of air from one region to another. Earth has winds that are fast and slow, hot and cold, wet and dry, high and low. All get started the same way.

The uneven heating of Earth's surface causes differences in air pressure. When air is warmed by nearby land or water, it spreads out and tends to rise, putting less (lower) pressure on Earth's surface. Cool air, which is more dense, tends to fall, putting more (higher) pressure on Earth's surface.

Over many centuries, powerful winds whittled the huge sandstone formations at Arches National Park, Utah *(below),* into surprising shapes.

Wind always moves from a high-pressure area, where cool air is sinking, to a low-pressure area, where warm air is rising. This weather map shows the location of both types of area (*H* is for high, *L* for low) on a given day. Lines called *fronts* form the boundaries of different air masses.

DID YOU KNOW . . . ?
Some experts say that wind can affect how people behave, even cause mental illness. In Italy, some people who committed crimes have blamed them on siroccos *(suh-ROK-ohs)*—strong winds that rise off the hot Sahara, a desert in northern Africa, and sweep north-ward over Italy and other countries on the Mediterranean Sea.

A barometer *(photo at right)* is a tool that measures air pressure. If a barometer shows decreasing air pressure, the weather is about to take a turn for the worse. The faster the decrease, the stormier it's likely to be.

Why is that so? Decreasing air pressure means that air is rising, exerting less pressure on Earth's surface. That rising air carries moisture that forms clouds. The heavier with moisture the clouds become, the more likely they are to drop rain.

BOTTLE BAROMETER

You can make a simple barometer that shows changes in air pressure. As air pressure increases, the air pushes down on the water in the glass, forcing it up the neck of your bottle barometer. As air pressure decreases, less water is forced into the bottle neck. The higher the air pressure, the higher the water in the bottle neck. The lower the air pressure, the lower the water in the bottle neck. If the water in the bottle neck falls quickly, watch for a storm!

What You'll Need
• a bottle with a long, narrow neck (an empty plastic ketchup bottle will do)
• a large drinking glass
• a ruler or measuring tape
• a permanent marker

What to Do
(1) Mark and number every half inch up the neck of the bottle. (2) Fill the bottle about halfway with water. (3) Hold your thumb over the bottle's mouth while standing it upside down in the glass. (When you let go, some water will run out into the glass.) The bottle's mouth should hang a little above the bottom of the glass.

Rest the bottle's sides on the rim of the glass.

Some water will run into the glass.

The bottle's mouth should not touch the bottom of the glass.

24

Large-scale Winds

Large-scale winds are high currents of air that blow over vast distances. About 30,000 to 35,000 feet above Earth, large rivers of cold air move in from the poles to clash with warmer air masses from the tropics, creating a huge stream of wind called a jet stream. Jet streams are Earth's fastest large-scale winds.

This long, narrow line of clouds shows the path of a high-speed jet stream crossing over Canada's Cape Breton Island.

The greater the difference in temperature between two air masses, the greater the difference in air pressure. The greater the air-pressure difference, the faster the winds. Winter jet streams over the Northern Hemisphere can blow up to 250 miles per hour!

Large-scale winds often follow regular patterns, as 15th-century sailors knew. To cross the Atlantic from Europe, sailors headed south into tropical waters until their sails caught the steady trade winds, which pushed them across to the Caribbean islands. To return, they sailed up the coast of North America to reach the westerlies—winds that pushed them back to Europe.

Earth's spin forces winds to curve as they blow across its surface. Winds arising north of the equator tend to curve to their right; those arising south of the equator tend to curve to their left. This force is called the Coriolis (*KORE-ee-OH-lus*) effect.

The white lines show the flow of large-scale winds over the Pacific Ocean.

Small-scale Winds

Q&A

Why is there often a cool breeze coming off the water at the beach on a hot day?

Land absorbs the sun's heat faster than water does. As warm air rises off the land, cooler air flows in off the water to replace it. This flow is called a sea breeze—a small-scale wind (one that blows over a small area).

The different heating and cooling rates of mountaintops and valleys can cause forceful winds. In southern California, warm, dry winds blow from the high desert to lower areas, such as Los Angeles. The winds get warmer and drier as they travel, parching grasses and shrubs in their path. In these dry conditions, a lightning strike or untended camp fire can lead to fast-spreading brush fires.

Measuring Speed and Direction

WIND

Sailors were probably the first to come up with ways to measure wind speed and direction. Their lives depended on being able to "read" the wind and weather.

Beaufort Scale

In 1805, a British admiral named Sir Francis Beaufort came up with a standard way to measure wind force by observing wave action at sea. His method—known as the Beaufort scale—was adapted for land, and has been used ever since.

Wind speed (mph)		Description	Effects on land
below 1		Calm	Smoke rises straight up
2-3		Light air	Smoke drifts slowly
4-7		Light breeze	Leaves rustle; wind vanes move
8-12		Gentle breeze	Flags ripple; leaves and twigs move
13-18		Moderate breeze	Leaves and dust fly; small branches move
19-24		Fresh breeze	Small trees sway
25-31		Strong breeze	Large branches sway; wind "whistles"
32-38		Near gale	Whole trees sway; difficult to walk into wind
39-46		Gale	Twigs break off trees
47-54		Strong gale	Branches break off trees
55-63		Whole gale	Trees uprooted; damage done to buildings
64-74		Storm	Extensive damage to landscape
above 74		Hurricane	Major destruction

One tool that meteorologists use to measure wind speed is the cup anemometer, invented about 150 years ago. Wind is caught by the cups, making them spin. By counting the rotations made in a specific amount of time, we can calculate how fast the wind is blowing.

A weather vane swings in the wind to show the direction from which the wind is blowing. In this photo, the wind is coming from the east.

STRONG CROSS WINDS

More than 1,500 years ago, Chinese weather watchers used wind socks to find wind direction and speed. A wind sock swings as the wind changes direction. The straighter it flies, the faster the wind.

Q&A
How fast can Earth's winds blow?
A tornado that hit central Oklahoma on May 3, 1999, had the fastest wind speed ever measured on Earth: 318 miles per hour!

29

Putting Wind to Work

Once we are able to measure wind's speed and direction, we can put it to work. Since ancient times, people have been coming up with new or better ways to do just that.

The big sail in front is called a spinnaker. Under the right wind conditions, this special sail can dramatically increase a sailboat's speed.

Using a hang glider, humans can ride the wind, like a bird with its wings outstretched.

Hot-air balloonists must know wind speed and direction, and try to predict how the weather will change during a flight. Hoping to set a new record by flying nonstop around the world, some balloonists fly high enough to use jet streams!

DID YOU KNOW . . . ?

A jet flying east from Chicago, Illinois, to New York City can save as much as 500 gallons of fuel if it flies in a jet stream with 150-mile-an-hour winds. The flight takes less time than the reverse trip.

People have been harnessing wind energy for centuries. In places that get steady-enough winds most of the year, windmills of old have been replaced by high-tech wind turbines like these. More than 15,000 such turbines make electricity for people living in southern California.

Why We Have Storms

Large air masses are constantly forming over land or water. Some are cold, some warm; some are wet, some dry—depending on the surface below. Upper-level winds push these air masses away from where they were formed. What happens when air masses of very different temperatures and air pressures meet? Often, we get a storm!

Some of the worst snowstorms strike in spring, when the sun's growing warmth creates strong winds that shove warm tropical air and cold polar air together with a bang.

Beyond this huge storm cloud, you can see clear skies. The downward streaks in the distance are falling rain.

The line where the two air masses meet is called a *front*. The term was coined by Norwegian meteorologists after World War I. The violent weather along weather fronts reminded them of military fronts, where armies clash on a battlefield.

DID YOU KNOW . . . ?

There is an old saying: "Cows lie down before a storm." Often, they do. Perhaps falling air pressure affects their digestive systems, so they stop grazing, or perhaps they lie down to keep their underparts dry. Cows' lying down is not a reliable weather predictor, however, as they may lie down for other unknown reasons.

When a warm front and cold front collide, clouds form above. A sudden clash can produce a dramatic line between clear sky and storm-brewing clouds.

Thunderstorms

Earth has more thunderstorms than any other kind of storm. About 40,000 crackle and zap around the world each day. Thunderstorms cover small areas—about 5 to 10 miles wide. They may or may not be part of a weather front.

3.

2.

1.

1. Warm, wet air rises from the ground in updrafts (upward-flowing air).

2. The air moves high enough to cool and form clouds, which continue to rise.

3. As high as 40,000 feet, water droplets in the clouds freeze into large ice crystals or form larger, heavier drops. These fall back through the clouds, creating powerful downdrafts (downward-flowing air).

4. A storm breaks out—heavy rain, thunder, and lightning occur. The more powerful the downdrafts, the more violent the storm.

5. After about an hour, the rain tapers off and the storm disappears.

4.

5.

If all the right conditions occur in the same place at the same time, a rainstorm can occur anywhere—even over a desert!

Rain-heavy clouds—one sign of an approaching thunderstorm—can darken skies, even at midday.

Thunderstorms happen most often in spring and summer. This is because they cannot develop without the unstable air caused by warm air rising into cold air above—a condition that occurs most often during those seasons.

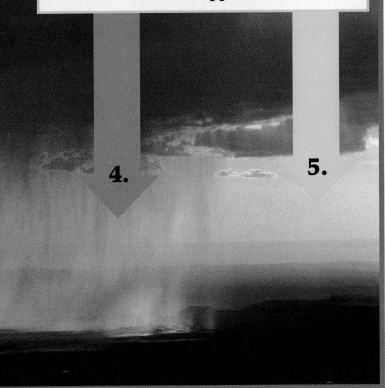

Lightning and Thunder

Lightning and electricity are the same thing: Benjamin Franklin *(below)* proved that in a 1752 experiment. He flew a kite into a thunderstorm. When lightning struck the kite, sparks flew from a metal key tied to the end of the string. Franklin was lucky—besides making a great discovery, he survived what could have been a fatal lightning strike.

Thor was the Norse god of thunder, war, and strength. He was said to throw a magic hammer to make thunderbolts fly from clouds.

A lightning bolt travels at about 60,000 miles per second, or one third the speed of light. It packs 30 million volts—enough electrical energy to power a city the size of New York!

1. Inside a storm cloud, updrafts and downdrafts blow water droplets or ice crystals back and forth against each other. This friction causes electrical charges to build up. (A similar thing happens when you rub an inflated balloon on your sweater sleeve.)

2. Positive charges (+) and negative (–) charges are attracted to each other. When opposite charges get strong enough, they slam together in a powerful bolt that we call lightning.

There are three types of lightning. *Cloud-to-ground* accounts for only one fourth of all lightning bolts. The rest are *cloud-to-cloud* or *cloud-to-air* lightning.

Q&A
How hot does lightning get?

Up to 54,000°F (29,982°C), more than five times as hot as the sun's surface! Moving at super-sonic speed, lightning makes the air expand and contract (heat and cool) very quickly. This makes sound waves that we hear as thunder.

When lightning strikes, one of the safest places to be is in a car with the windows rolled up. (The electricity will flow through the car's metal into the ground.) The most dangerous places outdoors include open ground or water. Indoors, stay away from plumbing, electrical wires, and phone lines. People have been killed by lightning in showers and bathtubs, and as they talked on the phone.

For centuries, sailors reported seeing a fiery glow at the tip of ships' masts when a thundercloud was directly overhead. They called it St. Elmo's fire, after the patron saint of sailors. Scientists think that it occurs when electrical forces inside a cloud are too weak to create a bolt, but strong enough to make sparks when they hit the top of a mast.

Don't hide under a tree during a thunderstorm! Lightning split this tree into splinters.

If someone tells you, "Lightning never strikes twice in the same place," don't believe it. Lightning—which always follows the easiest, most-direct route—has been proven to strike the same object more than once.

Most people are killed when struck by lightning, but some survive. This Virginia park ranger, Roy C. Sullivan, survived not one strike, but *seven* between 1942 and 1977!

39

Tornadoes

Whether you call them tornadoes, twisters, or whirlwinds, they pack the strongest winds on Earth. With winds that can whirl faster than 300 miles per hour, a tornado can flatten buildings—an entire town, even—in seconds.

The U.S. has some 1,000 tornadoes each year. They can happen at any time of the year, but most occur in April, May, and June in "Tornado Alley"—the central and southern parts of the Great Plains.

More tornadoes rip through Tornado Alley than any place else in the world.

Tornadoes often form when a thunderstorm's powerful, warm, wet updrafts come close to an unusually strong, central downdraft. If, at the same time, the wind hitting the top of the storm cloud is blowing in a different direction from the wind below, the storm system starts to rotate. It turns slowly at first, then faster and faster as the warm and cold air currents interact.

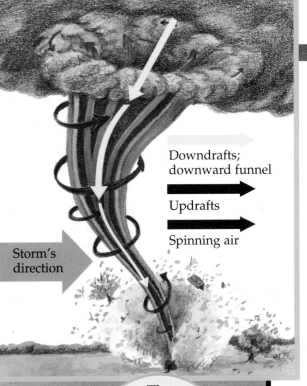

Downdrafts;
downward funnel

Updrafts

Spinning air

Storm's
direction

The funnel cloud of a tornado travels with the storm cloud at an average speed of 30 to 40 miles per hour. The funnel can be anywhere from 50 feet to a mile wide, and can damage areas from just a few yards wide to 100 miles long. Most tornadoes last less than 15 minutes.

The strongest spin is located at the center of the storm. As the tornado develops, this spin works its way down, like a strand of twisted rope, forming a funnel—and a powerful vacuum. The funnel cloud blackens and thickens as it touches ground and sucks up debris.

Fujita Tornado Scale

Scale number	Wind speed	Damage caused
F-0	Up to 72 mph	Light
F-1	73 to 112 mph	Moderate
F-2	113 to 157 mph	Considerable
F-3	158 to 206 mph	Severe
F-4	207 to 260 mph	Devastating
F-5	261 to 318 mph	Incredible

Meteorologists use the Fujita tornado scale to rank tornadoes' strength. The scale was developed in the late 1960s by Dr. T. Theodore Fujita, a tornado specialist.

In *The Wizard of Oz*, a tornado plucks up a farmhouse and carries Dorothy and Toto to Oz. Can a tornado really pick up and move a house? Yes, if its winds reach F-5 on the Fujita scale. In April 1974, a tornado lifted two school buses from an Ohio high school parking lot and dropped them inside the school.

Measurements and data gathered by daring storm chasers help scientists understand what causes tornadoes' deadly force.

Q&A
What was the world's deadliest tornado?
The Tri-State Tornado of March 18, 1925. It lasted for three and a half hours, cutting a path 219 miles long across Missouri, Illinois, and Indiana. It killed 695 people, injured 1,980, and left 11,000 homeless.

The period of April 3-4, 1974, holds the world's record for most tornadoes in 24 hours: 148. The so-called Super Outbreak wrecked more than 600 square miles in the United States and Canada, killing 315 people and causing $500 million in damages.

Can it really rain cats and dogs? Perhaps. In 1994, fish rained down on Australia's dry outback region! A waterspout had sucked them up, then dumped them over land. Waterspouts and tornadoes have been blamed for other "beastly" rains, such as frogs or shellfish.

Waterspouts are tornadoes that occur over oceans or large lakes, sucking up large amounts of water when the funnel touches the surface. As a waterspout weakens, it dumps a huge load of water, often damaging coastline property. The largest waterspout ever recorded, off the coast of Australia in 1898, was close to one mile high.

Many people believe that opening windows will keep a house from exploding in a tornado, but recent studies have proven that idea false. It is the force of a tornado's winds that destroys houses—not unequal air pressure.

44

Dust devils are whirlwinds caused by intense heating of dry ground, usually in desert areas. A rapid updraft of warm air starts a spin that can carry dust half a mile into the sky. *Jinniy*, the Arabic word for a dust devil, is the source of the mythical, wish-granting genie that escapes from its magic lantern in a whirlwind.

Hurricanes

Hurricanes are huge storms born over tropical waters. Meteorologists call them *tropical cyclones*. They are usually called *hurricanes* in the Atlantic Ocean and in the Pacific bordering North America, *typhoons* in the North Asian Pacific, and *cyclones* in the Indian Ocean and southern Pacific. These giant storms claim more human lives each year than any other kind of weather.

Formation of a Hurricane
(Red arrows indicate the flow of air.)

Thunderstorms often develop over tropical oceans. When conditions are right, several storms cluster, forming the vast spiral that we see in satellite photos. If that spiral's winds reach a speed of 74 miles per hour or above, it officially becomes a hurricane.

For a hurricane to form, four conditions must exist:
● ocean water that is at least 80°F (27°C)
● unstable air, with the right mix of high and low pressure
● strong winds high in the upper atmosphere that push smaller thunderstorms into an ever-tightening spiral until the storm twirls around a central "eye"
● winds of 74 miles per hour or faster

The Pacific has three times as many tropical cyclones a year as the Atlantic. Southern Asia is often hardest hit. In 1991, a tropical cyclone and storm surge battered the small country of Bangladesh, killing 125,000 people and leaving millions homeless.

A cyclone's devastating power reduced this home in Bangladesh to rubble.

A hurricane can last from several hours to several weeks and can cut paths of destruction 200 to 500 miles across. Hurricanes are rated on a scale of 1 to 5 using wind speed to measure intensity. The scale is used to estimate the storm's potential damage and flooding.

On August 29, 2005, New Orleans, LA was devastated by Hurricane Katrina, a category 4 hurricane (winds 131-155 mph). This U.S. Coast Guard boat is on a search and rescue mission.

Eye

A hurricane's heaviest rains and strongest winds (up to 200 miles per hour) are in the ring of clouds forming the "eye wall." The eye is the central column of calm, open air. When the eye passes overhead, the clear skies often fool people into thinking that the storm is over—until the storm's other side slams in.

Air pressure within a hurricane's eye is much lower than in the rest of the storm. A bulge of seawater forms beneath the low-pressure eye, like water being sucked up a straw. This bulge—called a storm surge—grows as the hurricane approaches land and makes huge waves.

This New Orleans neighborhood was still flooded two weeks after Hurricane Katrina hit.

Hurricane Katrina overwhelmed the levee system designed to protect New Orleans. Major damage to the coastal regions in Louisiana, Mississippi, and Alabama made Katrina the costliest natural disaster in U.S. history.

DID YOU KNOW . . . ?
The hurricane season runs from early summer to late fall. Hurricane Allison, which hit Florida on June 5, 2005, was the earliest hurricane to strike the U.S. in 120 years. The season's latest (which was not named) hit Florida on November 30, 1925.

Meteorologists use high-tech equipment to track a hurricane's path: radar, satellites, and computers, as well as planes that fly into hurricanes to measure their force. Even so, making accurate forecasts is difficult. Meteorologists consider themselves good at tracking a hurricane's path and "so-so" at predicting its strength, but poor at predicting its size.

Hurricane Georges, tracked September 18-28, 1998.

Forecasts are most accurate within 24 hours of a hurricane's arrival. A 24-hour warning may not give people enough time to leave a high-risk area. If a warning is given too soon, however, and the hurricane changes course, people may stop taking warnings seriously.

St. Thomas, U.S. Virgin Islands, after 1995's Hurricane Marilyn.

Meteorologists name hurricanes to avoid confusion when several develop in the same time period. Only female names were used from 1953 to 1978. Both male and female names have been used since 1979.

The Army helped distribute emergency supplies to Florida storm victims after 1992's Hurricane Andrew.

Blizzards

True blizzards occur less often than other types of storms. The National Weather Service defines a blizzard as a snowstorm with winds of at least 35 miles per hour, temperatures below 20°F (-4°C), and visibility of less than one quarter of a mile.

Some people say that a real blizzard occurs only once a century. That is not true, but blizzards *are* rather fussy. They demand high winds, low temperatures, and cloud conditions that bring heavy snowfall. Blizzards occur most often far inland, in winter and early spring.

Perhaps the most famous blizzard in U.S. history happened on March 11-14, 1888. Up to 58 inches of snow fell, crippling the northeastern U.S. The storm was blamed for hundreds of deaths from Virginia to New England, including 400 in New York City alone.

The Blizzard of '88: Howling winds whipped snow into drifts 20 feet high. This photo was taken on New York's Madison Avenue on March 14, 1888.

Q&A
What is a whiteout?

When a blizzard's combination of low cloud cover and falling snow make it impossible to see more than a few feet or even inches ahead. People who have been caught in a whiteout say that they couldn't tell the difference between the ground and the sky! This can be dangerous, especially for drivers, skiers, and mountain climbers.

How Clouds Form

When sunlight heats oceans, lakes, and rivers, some of the water evaporates, or changes from a liquid to a gas called water vapor. As warm air holding that vapor rises into the atmosphere, it cools. Cool air cannot hold as much water vapor as warm air, so the vapor condenses—it changes back to liquid form. Tiny water droplets form around dust particles as they hang in the air, and a cloud is born.

There is an old saying: "Every cloud has a silver lining." The "silver" is sunlight passing through the thin edges of an otherwise dense cloud. The denser the water or ice in a cloud, the darker it looks. The water or ice blocks the sunlight, giving most of the cloud a dark underside.

DID YOU KNOW . . . ?

On an average day, there are 40,000,000,000,000 (that's 40 *trillion*) gallons of water in the atmosphere over the U.S. alone! (That includes water vapor in the air, and water droplets and ice crystals in clouds.)

The air inside your lungs, warmed by your body heat, is full of water vapor. When you exhale on a cold day, that vapor hits the cold air outside and condenses into your own mini-cloud.

Kinds of Clouds

True weather watchers know their clouds. There are three basic types. To figure out which type is which, look at the shape.

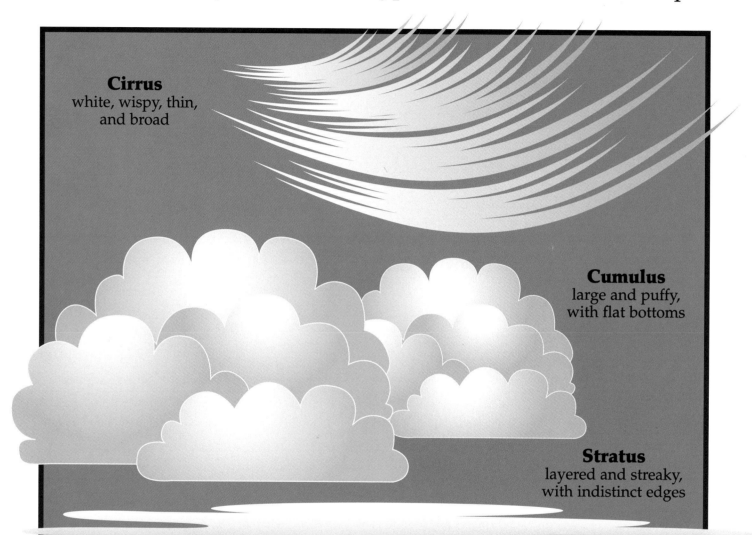

Cirrus
white, wispy, thin, and broad

Cumulus
large and puffy, with flat bottoms

Stratus
layered and streaky, with indistinct edges

In naming clouds, meteorologists use Latin words that describe how a cloud looks, how high above the ground it forms, and (sometimes) what it does. Adding certain prefixes or suffixes to a cloud's basic name tells you more about it.

Latin prefix or suffix:	means:
cirro- or *-cirrus*	curly
cumulo- or *-cumulus*	mass; in heaps
alto-	mid-level clouds
strato- or *-stratus*	spread out; layered
nimbo- or *-nimbus*	rain-producing

HIGH-LEVEL CLOUDS (20,000 feet or higher)

Clouds form and are found at different levels of Earth's atmosphere. These are some of the cloud types found at each level.

Cirrus

Cirrostratus

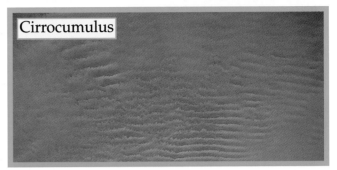
Cirrocumulus

MID-LEVEL CLOUDS (6,500 to 20,000 feet)

Altostratus

Altocumulus

LOW-LEVEL CLOUDS (below 6,500 feet)

Stratocumulus

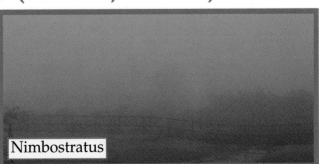
Nimbostratus

Stratus

Cumulus

What Clouds Tell Us

Once you can recognize different types of clouds, you can "read" them for clues about weather conditions. For instance, heaped-up cumulus clouds, which last only a short time, are a sign of rapidly rising warm air over a small area.

Fair-weather cumulus clouds may grow into a cumulonimbus cloud like this one. Cumulonimbus can tower from near the ground to as high as 60,000 feet—more than twice the height of Mount Everest! Cumulonimbus clouds, sometimes called thunderheads, carry thunderstorms. They can bring rain, snow, or hail. Tornadoes grow out of such storms.

58

Flat, layered stratus clouds, which can last for days, are a sign of a large, moist air mass that rose slowly. Stratus or strato-cumulus clouds can become so thick with water or ice that they darken the sky. They can thicken into nimbostratus clouds, which produce rain or snow.

WHICH CLOUDS DO WHAT

The cloud most likely to . . .

- **signal fair weather:** cumulus
- **bring rain, snow, or hail:** cumulonimbus
- **bring a tornado:** cumulo-nimbus
- **bring a long, steady rainfall or snowfall:** alto-stratus or nimbostratus
- **produce drizzle or mist:** stratus

Low-lying stratus clouds

These feathery "mare's tails" cirrus clouds are made entirely of ice crystals.

Cirrus, cirrostratus, and cirrocumulus clouds form high in the sky, where the air is very cold. Snow may form in these high clouds, but is not likely to reach the ground unless the air below is also cold and lower clouds are producing precipitation as well. Cirrostratus clouds usually signal an approaching storm.

Often, you see more than one kind of cloud in the sky. They form at different levels, where wind speeds, temperatures, and amounts of water vapor vary.

Most clouds form when warm air rises, but mammatus clouds form when cooling air sinks. These clouds, which look like clumps of rounded sacks, often form below cumulonimbus clouds.

High cirrus clouds may be blowing in one direction while lower cumulus clouds blow in another. The type headed your way can be a clue to weather coming up.

DID YOU KNOW . . . ?
What you don't see *can* hurt you! A dangerous thunderhead can move in behind low-level stratocumulus and mid-level altocumulus clouds, which block it from view. If you hear thunder with a mixed sky, consider it a warning and take shelter.

Fog

Fog is a cloud that forms near the ground and stays low. It can occur at different times, and can last for a long time or only briefly, as this weather saying suggests:

Evening fogs will not burn soon,
Morning fog will burn 'fore noon.

Dense, coastal fogs can limit visibility to 10 feet or less. They are dangerous to sailors because they block the light from lighthouses and buoys. To navigate, sailors listen for foghorns.

An early-morning fog over a pond or lake will not last long—the rising sun's warmth soon burns it off. This kind of fog forms when the sky is clear and there is little or no wind. The cold water cools the warm, moist air just above to its condensation point. You can see the heavy water droplets hanging in the air just above the water's surface.

Q&A
What is smog?

Fog that forms in smoky air. (**Sm**oke + f**og** = **smog**.) Smog is often thicker than fog because smoke puts more particles in the air, and droplets form around them when condensation takes place. Exhaust from vehicles and factories and soot from fires contribute to smog over major cities.

The fogs that blanket San Francisco's famous Golden Gate Bridge often linger for hours. The fogs form out over the Pacific Ocean, where warm air meets cold water currents, then are blown into San Francisco's bay area. The area's breezes and cool temperatures keep the fog from burning off quickly.

The Water Cycle

The next time you pour yourself a glass of water, think about this: The water molecules that you are about to drink are the same water molecules that were sloshing around when dinosaurs walked Earth!

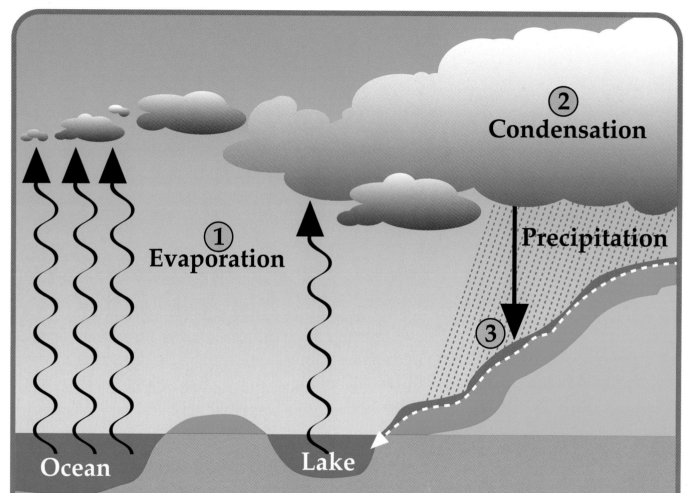

Ever since Earth was formed, water has passed from the oceans and land into the atmosphere and back again, in the continuous cycle shown here.

1. Water evaporates (becomes water vapor) and rises into the atmosphere.

2. When moist air cools, clouds form. The water vapor condenses (changes back to water droplets). The droplets fall from the cloud as rain or snow.

3. Rain or melted snow seeps underground or is channeled into rivers and flows back to the ocean.

65

Rain

What makes a cloud bring rain? When a cloud has enough water droplets to clump together, the drops get larger and larger until they are heavy enough to fall as rain. If the cloud-level air is cold enough, the ice crystals that form eventually get heavy enough to fall. When the ice melts as it falls, it rains; other-wise, it snows.

Water droplets within a cloud are tiny: about 0.02 millimeters across. The barely visible droplets that hang in fog or mist are that size. Droplets large enough to fall as rain range in size from 0.5 millimeters to 6 millimeters in diameter (across). This dot is 6 millimeters across: ● Any droplet larger than that would break apart as it fell through the air.

What do the words *drizzle* and *showers* mean to meteorologists?

Drizzle is the lightest kind of rain, with droplets just heavy enough to fall. Drizzle is sometimes part of a large weather system, and might fall steadily from stratus clouds.

Showers, on the other hand, are local events that fall from cumulus-type clouds. Showers come and go quickly. They may happen even in bright sunshine, or drench one side of a street while leaving the other side dry.

Q&A
Is there such a thing as red rain?

Yes! Sirocco winds, which blow over Africa's Sahara, sweep fine red dust high into the air, where it travels great distances. Eventually, water vapor condenses around that dust and falls—as red rain—in the Alps and other parts of Europe.

Rainbows

In many folk and fairy tales, there is something magical about rainbows. Their sudden, short-lived beauty can certainly take your breath away. Since they often come as bad weather is changing into good, they can lift your spirits as well.

The best time to see rainbows is when the sun is low in the sky, early or late in the day.

A rainbow is a combination of water and sunlight. Rainbows occur when there is rain falling in one part of the sky and the sun is shining in another part. If the sun hits all those droplets at the right angle, the light is bent by their curved surfaces—the same way a prism bends light. This breaks the light into those lovely bands of color.

To see a rainbow, you have to be standing with your back to the sun, looking toward where the rain is falling. No two people see the same rainbow, because even a slight change in position changes the angle of light on the droplets, affecting what is seen.

Sometimes, you can see two rainbows at once! A rainbow's colors always appear in the same order: red, orange, yellow, green, blue, indigo, and violet.

Not all cultures consider rainbows good luck. In one African folk tale, a rainbow is a giant snake that brings bad luck if it touches your house. In ancient Greece, a rainbow was called an *iris*, after the goddess who brought unrest and war.

Seasonal Rains

Seasonal winds that bring heavy rain are part of the normal weather pattern in some parts of the world. In Asia, for instance, seasonal winds often bring rains that are a welcome relief after six months of dry weather. However, some seasonal rains are too heavy to deal with, such as those dumped by tropical cyclones (called typhoons in Asia and hurricanes in North America).

Monsoon rains in Benares, India.

One of the wettest places in the world is Cherrapunji, India. It holds the world record for the most rain in a single time period: 192 inches in 15 days! The rain was part of the wet monsoon season that occurs in India every six months. Cherrapunji also holds the records for most rain in one month (366 inches) and most rain in one year (1,042 inches).

Above: Typhoons often cause floods, like this 1994 flood in Taiwan. So much rain falls at one time that rivers overflow and the ground cannot absorb the water.

In Bangladesh and parts of India, powerful cyclone winds can make the heavy rains even more devastating.

73.5".............
72"........

Areas with seasonal rains often have seasonal dry spells as well. This shrinking watering hole will swell again when the rainy season returns.

What is the most rain ever to fall in a 24-hour period? On March 15-16, 1952, 73.5 inches fell on Chilaos, Réunion (an island in the Indian Ocean). That was enough water to cover someone 6 feet (72 inches) tall!

Rain on Demand?

We depend on rain to provide the water that living things—plants, humans, and animals—need in order to survive. When we don't get enough of it, we seek ways to make more.

In 1915, San Diego, California, hired a rainmaker named Charles M. Hatfield to fill its reservoir. In January 1916, he burned chemicals atop a 28-foot tower. Within days, it rained—and kept raining, causing severe flooding. The city refused to pay Hatfield's $10,000 fee. The courts finally ruled that the rain was an act of God. The city did not have to pay Hatfield—but he could not be sued for flood damages, either.

Today, scientists can sometimes use a method called *cloud seeding* to force a cloud to drop rain. In cloud seeding, an airplane drops chemicals into clouds—chemicals that make the water vapor condense and fall. Cloud seeding can help people in areas suffering from severe water shortages—but only if the area has the proper type of cloud to work with.

People build irrigation systems to move water from a rainy area—like this wetland, for instance—to a dry one. However, this may cause problems in the wet area for the plants and animals whose survival depends on it.

Some Native American peoples, especially those living in drier parts of the Great Plains or the Southwest, performed rain dances to please spirits with the power to make it rain.

Rain as Environment

Since rain is so important to living things, it is not surprising that rain forests—which average more than 100 inches of rain in a year—are home to more different kinds of life than any other environment.

The tiny poison-dart frog (about the size of your littlest finger-nail!) relies on the moist air of South American rain forests to keep its skin healthy. It lays its eggs in small pools of water that collect at the base of certain plants.

Rain forests *(in green on map)* cover less than 10 percent of Earth's land area, yet they support at least half of all plant and animal species.

The tallest rain-forest trees form a canopy that absorbs 99 percent of the sunlight. Everything living below that canopy survives on filtered light—and the high levels of humidity.

Most rain forests are near the equator, where the sun's rays are direct year-round. The combination of stea warmth and heavy moisture helps plants grow quickly

Dew and Frost

Sometimes, water vapor in low-lying air condenses on spider webs, grass, or other surfaces, making tiny dew-drops that glisten in the early-morning sun.

We usually see dew after a still night when the sky was clear. Dew forms when the ground and other outdoor surfaces get cold enough during the night to make the air's moisture condense.

WORDS FOR THE WISE

Dew point is a meteorologist's term for the temperature at which dew starts to form—when moist air can hold no more water.

Some desert animals depend on dew for the water they need to survive—this Namibian darkling beetle, for instance. Once dew has formed on its body, it stands on its head—then drinks the dew drops that slide down to its mouth.

When it is cold enough, condensing water vapor freezes to form frost instead of dew. Frost forms when moisture changes directly from vapor to ice crystals (gas to solid), without making water drops first. These ice crystals grow into feathery patterns, which you may see on window panes or car hoods.

DID YOU KNOW . . . ?
You might see dew or frost without fog, but you will never see fog without dew or frost!

Frostbite is an injury to skin left unprotected in very cold, often windy weather. The moisture in thin-skinned areas—especially the nose, ears, toes, and fingers—freezes, making the skin tingle, then go numb. Frostbite is serious! Get help from someone experienced in first aid. If not treated promptly and properly, frostbite can cause serious damage to skin and blood vessels. In the worst cases, damaged fingers or toes must be **amputated** (cut off).

77

Floods

Any time there is a heavy rain, people in low-lying areas—especially near waterways—start watching for rising water. A flood can happen quickly and last only a few hours, or develop slowly and last for weeks. Either way, floods are blamed for more property damage worldwide than any other kind of weather-related disaster.

This is the control tower of the airport at Jefferson City, Missouri—hidden below five feet of floodwater on June 9, 1993.

In 1993, for the first time that people could remember, the Mississippi and Missouri rivers topped their banks at the same time. This created the "Great Mississippi Flood"—the costliest and longest-lasting U.S. flood of the 20th century. In three months, the two rivers flooded more than 16,000 square miles in nine states, causing $20 billion in property damage and 48 deaths.

The Great Mississippi Flood of 1993 was caused by heavier-than-normal snowfalls the winter before, then heavier-than-normal rains in the spring and summer. All that water had no place to go except into the rivers—and over their banks.

This 1993 flood in northeastern Bangladesh took some 220 lives.

Floods are often caused by hurricanes, especially in coastal areas where storm surges add to heavy rainfall. When a cyclone hit Bangladesh in 1991, most of the 150,000 deaths it caused were flood-related.

Flash Floods

Sometimes, when a lot of rain falls in a short period of time, a river or stream rises very quickly, causing a flash flood. This is common in narrow canyons or gorges, which force the extra water to rush from high ground to low. Flash floods happen so fast, it isn't always possible to warn people downstream.

A flash flood can strike on a sunny day when there is no sign of rain. The water rushes into a low-lying area—like this Texas highway— from a downpour many miles away.

Above:
More than 2,200 people were killed in the Johnstown Flood. On May 31, 1889, after unusually heavy rains, a dam gave way, sending 20 million tons of water roaring down a narrow valley. By the time the water reached Johnstown, Pennsylvania, an hour later, it was a 30-foot-high wall. It wiped out the center of town within 10 minutes.

Heavy rains or flood-water can sweep tons of mud with it, setting off destructive mud slides—like the one that swamped this California home.

DID YOU KNOW . . . ?
In the deserts of south-western U.S., more people die by drowning than by dehydration (serious dryness of body tissues). They drown in flash floods that take them by surprise.

Droughts

Drought *(rhymes with OUT)* is a dry period during which an area gets less rainfall than usual. A drought area's natural plant and animal life often suffer from the dryness—and will die off if the drought continues for too long.

Two drought victims—earth and animal—in South Africa's Kalahari National Park.

In 1982 and 1983, rains that usually fall over eastern Australia in winter and spring never arrived because El Niño—a warmer-than-usual area of water in the Pacific Ocean—changed wind patterns. Huge dust storms and wildfires damaged many areas.

Drought in the Great Plains, along with overfarming and overgrazing, led to the devastating "Dust Bowl" of the 1930s. Many farmers were ruined as once-rich farmland dried up and blew away.

The Dust Bowl was not the longest rainless period in U.S. history. That record is held by Bagdad, California, which had 767 rainless days between October 3, 1912, and November 8, 1914.

Q&A
What is a dust storm?
During a long-term drought, topsoil crumbles into a powdery dust. Dry winds may then cause a dust storm, which can sweep tons of soil as high as 10,000 feet into the air and carry it several thousand miles away.

This soil—now so dry that huge cracks have formed in it—was once the bed of a lake.

A type of cloud, called pyrocumulus, can form above wild-fires. (*Pyro-* means "fire.") These clouds are created by the hot, rising air and moisture from burning plants. Pyrocumulus clouds can make lightning that starts more wildfires. They also can make rain that helps put fires out.

When rain finally does come to a drought-stricken area, it can be more a cause of worry than relief. If the dry ground is too hard to soak up moisture, a downpour can cause severe flooding.

DID YOU KNOW . . . ?

● Arica, Chile, holds the world record for the longest rainless period: 14 years (October 1903 to January 1918).

● Chile's Atacama Desert is considered to be the driest place on Earth. It gets an average of only 0.003 inches of rain a year.

This helicopter is dropping water on a wildfire in California's often-dry Sierra Nevada mountain range.

Drought-dried vegetation can become fuel for wildfires. Most wildfires are started by lightning or people who are careless with cigarettes or campfires. Wildfires are most common in places where hot, dry winds and high summer temperatures often cause drought.

Snow

Above:
Snowflakes and ice crystals photographed through an electron microscope, a modern device that enables us to see extremely small objects.

When the temperature inside a cloud is below 32°F (0°C), tiny ice crystals form. If those crystals clump and freeze together, they make snowflakes. The flakes keep growing until they are heavy enough to fall. If the air that they fall through is cold enough, they reach the ground as snow.

Depending on the air temperature, one inch of rainfall—if it freezes—can equal from 10 to 40 inches of snow! (The lower number is for wet, slushy snow; the higher number, for dry, powdery snow.)

No one knew how snowflakes are structured until the microscope was invented. A farmer named William Bentley (1865-1931) came up with the theory that no two snowflakes are alike—after magnifying and photographing thousands of them.

Q&A
Are snowflakes always six-sided?
Often, but not always. Snowflakes may also be triangular, or frozen in the shape of columns or needles.

These are computer-enhanced versions of Bentley's photos. Snowflakes vary because the temperature and humidity when they form also vary, even if only slightly.

Cold air carries less moisture than warm air. If air is really cold, it can't hold enough moisture for snow to form. That is why more snow falls in parts of the U.S. and Canada than at the North or South poles, where it is often too cold to snow.

A snowy day in Washington, D.C.

The world record for the most snow measured in a single snowfall season belongs to Mount Baker, Washington. It got 1,140 inches (95 feet) of the white stuff during its 1998-1999 snowfall season! The previous record was 1,122.5 inches (93.5 feet) at Mount Rainier, Washington, in 1971-1972.

Knowing snow helps this Inuit family get around in northern Canada.

WORDS FOR THE WISE
The Inuit, who live in Alaska and northern Canada, have different names for different kinds of snow. Here are a few:
- *aniu* (an-ee-YOO): falling snow
- *pukak* (poo-KAK): avalanche snow
- *apun* (a-PYUN): snow on the ground
- *qaliq* (kah-LEEK): snow on trees
- *mauja* (mow-YAH): deep, soft snow
- *upsik* (OOP-sik): packed snow

植村直己物語

People who live where there is a lot of snow often get creative with it. These snow and ice sculptures were part of an annual snow festival in Hokkaido, Japan.

An avalanche—when a large section of snow suddenly tumbles down a mountainside—can be deadly to hikers, skiers, and snowboarders. It happens when a lot of fresh snow piles up on a base of hard-packed snow or ice. Anything can set it off; sudden noises, warm sunshine, and shifting winds are common triggers.

An avalanche can dump as much as 100,000 tons of snow, moving 60 to 200 miles per hour.

The horse-drawn sleigh, a centuries-old way of travel, can be more effective than any motor vehicle on snow-covered roads. In bygone days, people welcomed snow-packed roads: The slippery surface was preferable to the rocks, ruts, and mud that plagued roads the rest of the year.

A heavy snow can leave snowdrifts that block miles of roadways, stranding motorists. Snow plows can clear the way, but take time and can be costly.

Q&A
Why are tall mountains often snowcapped?

Mountains force warm winds upward, where they cool, and where the moisture they carry forms clouds. The higher you go, the thinner and cooler the air. This means that conditions are often right for snow to form and fall on mountain peaks.

Hail, Ice, and Sleet

Snow is not the only cold stuff that falls from clouds.

Hailstones (*below and at left*) are usually pea-size, but can be the size of oranges or even larger.

Hailstones—frozen balls of ice—are produced inside cumulonimbus clouds during thunderstorms. Hail forms when small bits of ice are swept through the supercooled water in a cloud. The ice grows until it is heavy enough to fall. This can happen even in hot weather, if the cloud is cold enough.

92

Rime (rhymes with TIME) is a crust of ice that forms on objects when the moisture in fog or a cloud is cooled so quickly that condensing water droplets freeze onto the nearest surface—like everything at this weather station on Mount Washington, New Hampshire.

Sleet is rain that freezes as it falls. This coats everything with a shimmering layer of ice that can be beautiful— but ice storms are deadly to trees and dangerous to anyone near branches or power lines that collapse under the ice's weight.

Where We Fit In

What we do and how we live affects Earth's atmosphere, and changes in Earth's atmosphere affect the weather.

Solar energy

Greenhouse gases in the atmosphere

Solar energy trapped as heat

The gases in Earth's atmosphere act like the glass in a greenhouse. Sunlight passes through, then is trapped close to Earth's surface, keeping it warm. This heat-trapping process is known as the greenhouse effect.

Exhaust from power stations, factories, and motor vehicles dumps high levels of carbon dioxide and other gases into the atmosphere. Some scientists think that these pollutants are increasing the greenhouse effect, raising Earth's temperature higher than nature alone would.

When rain mixes with industrial pollution, it can become as acidic as lemon juice— more than 10 times as acidic as normal rain. Acid rain weakens and kills plant life, sometimes destroying entire forests. It also damages buildings and monuments.

Acid rain damaged these trees as well as the statue above.

If an increased greenhouse effect really is making Earth's climate warmer, it could spell big trouble for the future. Melting just part of Antarctica's vast, two-mile-thick ice cap could raise the global sea level by about 17 feet, putting many coastal cities—including New York, Sydney, and London—under water.

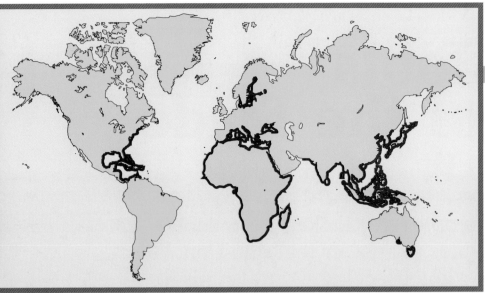

The red lines on the map above show coastal areas most likely to suffer serious flooding and storm-surge damage by the 2080s if the seas continue to rise.

In the past 100 years, the global sea level rose 4 to 6 inches. In the next century, it could rise even higher: 6 inches to 3 feet! That may not sound like much, but a global sea-level rise of just 3 feet would mean that:

- The Netherlands would lose 6 percent of its land area.
- Bangladesh would lose 17.5 percent of its land area.
- About 80 percent of the Majuro Atoll, a group of islands in the Pacific Ocean, would be completely covered by water.
- Low-lying coastal cities would be flooded, and pounded by storm surges during cyclones and other storms.

Heavy rains caused this street in the Netherlands to flood—but if seas keep rising, parts of the Netherlands could be like this every day.

Tools of the Trade

What will tomorrow's weather be like? For centuries, people have looked for reliable ways to answer that question. From observing natural signs to developing high-tech satellites, we have found many ways—some more reliable than others.

Woolly bear caterpillar

According to one old saying, "The wider the woolly bear's middle brown band, the milder the coming winter." Some scientists once compared woolly bear caterpillar bands with winter temperatures. They matched! The study was not broad enough, however, to prove whether the saying is reliable beyond those particular caterpillars at that particular time.

"Red sky at night, sailors delight; red sky at morning, sailors take warning" is another weather-prediction saying. It often works in the mid-latitudes of North America, where weather systems usually move from west to east.

We can tell the age of most trees by counting the rings formed as the trunk grows. Each pair of rings represents one year. (The light-colored ring shows early-season growth; the darker ring, late-season growth.) The rings also reveal what the weather was like: The wider the light ring, the better the weather for growth.

WEST

DUSK

EAST

DAWN

The sky looks red when the sun is low in the sky and its light is filtered by clouds. So a red dusk can mean that the clouds overhead—and bad weather—are moving away from us, while a red dawn can mean they are coming our way.

Scientists can tell what weather trends were like centuries ago by studying the trunks of ancient trees.

A few centuries ago, people began inventing instruments to observe weather changes. Leonardo da Vinci (1452-1519) designed a hygrometer that used paper disks to measure how much moisture was in the air. Galileo Galilei (1564-1642) invented a thermometer to measure air temperature—now the world's most common weather instrument.

Evangelista Torricelli (1608-1647)—one of Galileo's students—invented the first barometer to measure air pressure.

This dome houses a Doppler radar antenna. Doppler radar tracks the movement of precipitation—where it is, in which direction it is headed, how fast it is moving, and how heavily it is falling.

Radar helps meteorologists make important short-term forecasts—such as how much rain a thunderstorm is producing, which helps them issue flash-flood warnings if needed. Radar's reliability has greatly reduced the number of false alarms.

100

Satellites observe weather changes on a large scale. Satellites thousands of miles above the equator track weather over North America and watch for storms. Lower-altitude satellites measure temperatures in different layers of the atmosphere and relay the information to ground-based weather stations.

Weather & You

You don't need high-tech tools to observe and predict the weather. With a few simple tools and a little practice, you may be able to make forecasts that match—or even beat—the experts'!

You can do a lot with four basic instruments and a notebook. Put the instruments where you can easily make regular observations (once or twice a day) and record them in your weather log.

- an outdoor thermometer
- a wind sock
- a bottle barometer
- a rain gauge and ruler
- a notebook to use as a weather log (*example at left*)

Weather Log

Date	Oct. 28, 2000
Time	8 a.m.
Temperature	42°F
Cloud cover	Clear
Wind speed	8-12 mph (or draw a picture of your wind sock)
Wind direction	SE
Barometer reading	(note the number of the line on your bottle barometer)
Rainfall	none

Make a Rain Gauge

Use an empty coffee can or other flat-bottomed, straight-sided container. Set it in an open place where it will not get knocked over. After a rain, measure the water's depth with a ruler and record the amount in your notebook. (Then empty the can for the next rainfall.)

Make a Wind Sock

Cardboard ring

What You'll Need
- a narrow, heavy-duty plastic bag (longer than it is wide), with both ends open
- plastic streamers, about 18 inches long
- a 1-inch-wide strip of cardboard (its length should be twice the width of the plastic bag)
- a stapler
- 3 pieces of kite string, each 12 inches long
- a large paper clip
- a long pole

What to Do
(1) Staple the cardboard strip to make a ring. (2) Slide this ring into one opening of the bag, fold the edge of the bag over it, and staple it in place. (3) Thread the strings between the ring and bag, evenly spaced, and knot them. Tie the other end of the strings to a paper clip. (4) Attach the streamers to the bag's free end. (5) Attach the paper clip end of your wind sock to the top of the pole. Make sure that the wind sock can swing freely. Mount the pole outside, where the sock can catch the wind. (6) Use a compass to note the wind direction: north, south, east, or west. (Remember: *Wind direction* is the direction the wind blows *from*, not *to*.)

- In your weather log, note which way the wind blows from most often. That is called the *prevailing wind*. Keep track of what kind of weather your area's prevailing wind is most likely to bring.
- Use the Beaufort scale with your wind sock to estimate wind speed.

Make a Cloud

To see how clouds form as warm air cools, try this simple activity:

What You'll Need:
- a clear glass jar with lid
- hot tap water
- 3-4 ice cubes

What to Do
Pour the hot water into the jar. (Be careful not to burn yourself!) Wait a few moments to let the water heat the air in the jar, then pour most of it out. Quickly place the lid on top of the jar, upside down, and set the ice cubes in the lid. Watch as misty clouds swirl downward from the lid into the jar!

The streaky lower part of this massive cloud is being pushed by wind from mountain updrafts, but the towering upper part is sitting in calmer air.

Glossary

Acid rain: rain mixed with air pollutants that is more acidic than normal rain. It can damage plant and animal life as well as buildings and statuary.

Air pressure: the weight of the atmosphere over a unit area of Earth's surface. Also called *barometric pressure*, air pressure is measured with a barometer.

Atmosphere: Earth's blanket of air. The atmosphere is divided into five different layers. The lowest layer, the *troposphere*, is where most of our weather occurs.

Aurora borealis (or northern lights): shimmering curtains of color seen in northern skies, caused by solar particles interacting with Earth's atmosphere. In the Southern Hemisphere, it is called **aurora australis** (or southern lights).

Blizzard: a heavy snowstorm with gale-force winds, temperatures below 20° F (below -6.7°C), and visibility of less than one fourth of a mile.

Climate: long-term weather conditions, especially temperature and rainfall amounts, that are typical of a region over many years.

Condensation: when water changes from a gas to a liquid. Condensation is necessary for a cloud to form. (See also DEW POINT, EVAPORATION, and WATER VAPOR.)

Coriolis effect: the curved path of high-level winds caused by Earth's spinning. Winds curve to the right in the Northern Hemisphere and to the left in the Southern Hemisphere. Weather systems tend to follow these paths.

Dew: tiny water droplets that form on the ground or other outdoor surfaces. Dew forms when objects get cold enough during the night to make the air's moisture condense. **Dew point** is the temperature at which water vapor in the air condenses to form water.

Drought: an unusual dry spell during which less than normal rain falls in a region.

El Niño: a warm ocean current flowing from the equator down the coast of South America. Especially warm or large El Niños cause unusual weather patterns worldwide.

Evaporation: when water changes from a liquid to a gas (water vapor).

Fog: a cloud that forms at ground level. When fog is polluted with smoke and soot, it is called *smog*.

Front: the boundary between two air masses of different temperatures and humidity. Most significant weather events happen along fronts.

Frost: ice crystals that form on cold outdoor surfaces when water vapor in the air condenses directly to ice (from a gas to a solid) without making liquid water first.

Global warming: an overall rise in the temperature of Earth's atmosphere. It may be caused by pollution that increases the amount of greenhouse gases, trapping more of the sun's heat than normal. (See GREENHOUSE EFFECT.)

Greenhouse effect: the overall warming of Earth caused by gases, especially carbon dioxide, in Earth's atmosphere. The gases trap some of the sun's heat, like a greenhouse's glass roof, and radiate it back to Earth.

Hail: balls of layered ice that form in the super-cooled updrafts of thunderstorms.

Humidity: the amount of water vapor in the air. Humidity is measured with a *hygrometer*.

Hurricane (also called *tropical cyclone* or *typhoon*): a huge, intense storm with winds of 74 miles per hour or faster, born over tropical waters from a cluster of thunderstorms.

Jet stream: Earth's fastest large-scale wind, flowing in a steady current about 30,000 to 35,000 feet above Earth. Jet streams are caused by huge, polar air masses clashing with tropical air masses.

Meteorologist: a scientist who specializes in the study and forecasting of weather.

Monsoon: a wind that reverses direction twice each year, causing two seasons, rainy and dry. The heaviest monsoon rains are in southern Asia and around the Indian Ocean.

Radar: an instrument that sends and receives radio waves, used to locate objects that will reflect the waves. Radar helps meteorologists find areas of heavy rainfall.

Rain: water drops heavy enough to fall from a cloud. Raindrops range in size from 0.5 to 6 millimeters across. Anything larger will break apart as it falls.

Sleet: rain that freezes as it falls from a cloud or when it hits a cold surface.

Snow: tiny ice crystals that clump together inside clouds until they are heavy enough to fall. Temperatures inside and around the clouds must be below freezing for snow to reach the ground.

Storm: a powerful weather system that forms when two different air masses clash, producing a mix of high winds and rain, snow, sleet, or hail.

Thunderstorm: a storm caused by rapidly rising warm, wet air that produces winds, rain, lightning, and thunder.

Tornado: a powerful, violent whirlwind that funnels down from a cumulonimbus cloud, with winds that can whirl faster than 300 miles per hour.

Waterspout: a whirlwind that drops from a cumulonimbus cloud and sucks up water from oceans or large lakes.

Water vapor: water in a gaseous form. When water evaporates, it becomes water vapor and mixes with air.

Weather: the general condition of Earth's air, including its temperature, moisture, wind speed, and cloud cover.

Wind: the movement of air from a high-pressure area to a low-pressure area.

Index

Picture Credits